W9-CPZ-249

CLASS _____   C/L

ACC

Eberle, Harold.

(LAST NAME OF AUTHOR)

Grace, the power to reign

(BOOK TITLE)

DATE DUE	ISSUED TO
5/03/-11	SHARON ANDREWS

CODE 4386-02, CLS-2, Broadman & Holman Publishers

Grace

The Power
to Reign

THE LIGHT SHINING FROM ROMANS 5-8

Harold R. Eberle

Worldcast Publishing
Yakima, Washington

Grace...the Power to Reign
The Light Shining from Romans 5-8

© 2001 by Harold R. Eberle
First Printing, June 2001
Second Printing, November 2008

Worldcast Publishing
P.O. Box 10653
Yakima, WA 98909-1653 USA
509-248-5837
email: office@worldcastpublishing.com
Web Site: www.worldcastpublishing.com

ISBN 1-882523-19-9
Cover by Eugene M. Holmes
Cover photo of R.D. Smith

Credits and Thanks

In addition to the many teachers and mentors who have helped me understand principles of living the victorious Christian life, I want to thank the individuals who have labored over these pages. James Bryson helped me change my style of writing from a toilsome teacher into a more acceptable form, enjoyable to everyone. Pastor Floyd Dahl deserves credit for adjusting my understanding of the place of the Law in the Christian's life. I also want to thank my students at Destiny Bible College for their input, especially Henk and Marjolein van Diest, and Ruth Johnson. As always, Annette Bradley is my final editor and she is the greatest. My wife, Linda, and Jane Johnson not only do the secretarial work, but also keep me going in life and ministry. Thank you.

Table of Contents

Introduction

Deep in my heart I believed that God did not want us living as defeated people. It simply did not make sense that God would forgive our sins, make us His children, and then abandon us to fight sin, temptations, and trials without His help and grace. I knew there had to be more power available.

I sought the Scriptures for answers—answers that had not been taught in the many churches I had attended, in the seminary at which I studied, nor in the numerous Christian books I had read. I was confident that God must have explained it somewhere in His Word.

The answers I sought began to unfold as I labored over Paul's book to the Christians in Rome. Once I began to see them, the related truths seemed to leap off of the pages. God does have power available for you and me to live victoriously. It became so obvious that I could not understand how these truths previously had been hidden from me.

Please allow me to share this with you. Let me take you through Romans, chapters five through eight, to view these passages in ways which you never may have seen them before. Once you see the truths in these chapters, they will leap off of the pages of your Bible, too.

Today I can say that there is no teaching which has changed my personal life so profoundly as the one explained in these pages. I pray you will be able to say the same thing.

DESPERATELY
SEARCHING FOR HELP

1

Church was boring. After four years in a little town in the northwest United States, each Sunday seemed more routine. Tragically, I was the pastor.

It was not like that when Linda (my wife) and I first started to lead the church. In the beginning, everything was a challenge. Living in a beautiful ski resort town in the mountains, people frequently came to our area to avoid the typical lifestyle of work and raising a family. Many young, unemployed, society drop-outs found their way to our church. New people were showing up every Sunday, and many came from difficult life situations. Church was exciting!

However, as the years went by, things became more settled and dignified. The young people matured. Normal families—those with jobs—started attending the church. As the congregation grew, we became comfortable and more socially acceptable.

Of course, there were many positive aspects to our growth, but I began to miss the free-spirited individuals who used to show up at church. I wanted to see more people come out of serious problems and step onto a road to victory. So I began to pray. I prayed especially for the people in my town who *really* needed help. Of course, everyone needs some help, but I was concerned about individuals who were in serious bondage to sin. I wanted to see God set them free.

Being a pastor in a small town (about 4,000 people), most of the locals knew me. I didn't know all of their names, but I could recognize the visible ones. Twelve individuals stood out as needing God's touch more than others. I began to pray for those twelve. A deep compassion filled my heart. I began to think of them lovingly as my "dirty dozen."

Church life went on as usual and I continued to pray. Then one evening I decided to reach out to those dozen individuals who had found their way into my heart. I went to some of their homes. I telephoned others. Then I walked the streets and entered the local bars to find the rest. During my visit with each of them, I asked each one to come visit me later that night in a church-owned apartment where I was going to minister to them personally. It must have been the grace of God, because that first night all twelve showed up.

In that room, six of the twelve sitting in front of me had spent time in jail. At least two of them had been in prison for murder. Another had spent time behind bars for armed robbery. Ten were men and two were women. One man for years had given himself to bizarre sexual perversions. One woman was a practicing lesbian. Two nights earlier one had tried to commit suicide. That night, as they all waited to hear what I had to say, it was obvious that several were drunk or high on drugs.

4

I taught on the love of God. I spent two hours pouring out my heart and doing everything I could to convince them that God loves them, in spite of anything they had done. I showed them from the Bible how God's love is based on His nature, not our failures or successes. I explained that it did not matter how many times they had been in jail or committed adultery. I talked to them about God's willingness to forgive any and every sexual sin. I told them that God wanted to love each of them as they always had wanted to be loved. At the end of our evening together, they all bowed their heads and joined me in a prayer to receive God's love and forgiveness.

That was not only a new start for them, it was a new beginning for me.

Two evenings later I reached out to the same twelve. I went and got them. Just because they had prayed a prayer did not mean they were instantly freed of their sin problems. I found them in their homes, I walked the streets, and I searched the same bars. I collected all twelve and gathered them back into our church apartment.

That second night I taught them about God's Holy Spirit and how they could be freed of sin. I had brought with me that evening some cigarettes and a bottle of vodka. At one point I poured a glass of vodka and told them—with all the passion I could muster—how God could set them free. As I threw the glass out a nearby open window, some of the men looked on with longing eyes. I hoped that they soon would be longing for

5

God with similar earnestness.

I finished that evening praying for each one that they might receive an empowering of God's Holy Spirit. Until that night, some of them could not even imagine God's willingness to reach down to them. They actually wanted help, but previously had no hope. For me, it was worth everything to see a glimmer of light in their eyes realizing that perhaps God really did care.

Within a week, I went out to gather those same twelve. We called the group "Overcomers," because that identified our goal. We came together not just for two or three meetings but several times each week for an extended period.

I loved those twelve. I desperately wanted to see them freed of their bondages. I wanted to see them know God more intimately and walk in His power.

However, during that season of my life, I was fighting not only for them, but for myself, as well. I was just as enslaved to my own sins as they were to theirs. Below the outward face of this pastor was a man buried in depression and tormenting thoughts—struggles I'd had for years, and only with God's help was I able to keep contained. I hated myself for being weak and beaten, always having to restrain a whirlwind of negative thoughts. I did not like what it did to my marriage or my walk with God. I was angry inside, and I was ashamed that in truth I was less than the man of God which people believed I was.

Working with those dozen struggling souls gave me hope. I knew if they could find freedom, then I could also.

I read books. I talked to others. I prayed. When one brother was sentenced to go through a state-run drug-and-alcohol-treatment program, I volunteered to stand by him and submit to the family-treatment portion of the program. I sought God for each of them—but even more for myself. We incorporated truths from every avenue available, including psychology, inner healing, and demon deliverance. Many things helped, but it was searching through the book of Romans that made God's answers clear to me.

CONTRASTING ADAM AND JESUS

2

In the book of Romans, the apostle Paul laid out truths in a very logical, step-by-step manner. The first four chapters focus on the fact that we are all sinners, and that we all need a Savior, Who is Jesus Christ. Paul explained how we are forgiven of our sins and justified when we put our faith in Jesus Christ. That is the starting point.

The people with whom I was working all were aware of their sins. I was aware of my weaknesses, too. We established in our minds the truth of the forgiveness available through Jesus Christ. It was *power over sin* for which we now were searching.

That is what Paul goes on to teach in Romans, chapters five through eight. In order to understand Paul's teaching here, we must recognize a basic comparison he makes between the power that came into the world through Adam and what came through Jesus Christ.

Referring to Adam, Paul writes:

> *Therefore, just as through one man sin entered into the world, and death through sin, and so death spread to all men, because all sinned—* (Rom. 5:12)

When Adam sinned, sin came into the world. Death found its access through sin. Then death spread to all of mankind.

Before we go on to explain what came into the world because of Jesus, note the *power* of sin and death: as people yield to the power of sin, they die. "For the wages of sin is death..." (Rom. 6:23). The death of which is spoken here is not only the final loss of life when we leave this earth, but the severing of man from the life of God. Such death is an ongoing process which constantly wears on us, weakening us both naturally and spiritually.

This death works hand in hand with sin. As death weakens each person, they find it even harder to resist the power of sin. Paul explained that sin *reigns* in death (Rom. 5:21). Death weakens individuals so they cannot conquer sin, and then, the consequence of sin is the increased force of death (Rom. 6:23; James 1:15). Paul refers to this tandem work as "the law of sin and death" (Rom. 8:2). As the law of gravity holds every person to this earth, so also there is a law causing all people to sin and yield to the forces of death. As a king rules over people, so also sin and death have a rulership position over humanity.

Sin & Death
Reign

To provide freedom from and victory over the power of sin and death, God sent Jesus. This is what Paul wanted the Christians in Rome—and you and me—to understand. Paul contrasts the negative forces released through Adam with the positive forces released through Jesus Christ. As sin and death came through Adam, grace and life came through Jesus (Rom. 5:12-17).

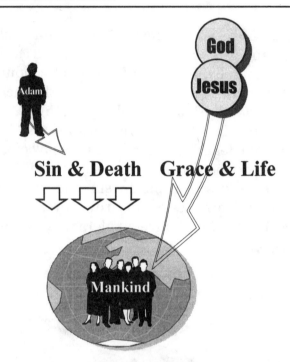

Every human being experiences the negative power of sin and death. It reigns. However, not all of us have experienced the power which flows through the life of Jesus Christ.

Of course, all Christians have put their faith in Jesus, and hence, experienced an initial burst of grace which brought them into forgiveness and a relationship with God. However, few have come to a revelation concerning how that power which flows through Jesus can be experienced on a consistent, on-going basis. This power is what Paul wanted all Christians to discover and access.

GOD IS
THE GIVER

3

Now I can discuss my favorite verse in the Bible:

> *For if by the transgression of the one, death reigned through the one, much more those who receive the abundance of grace and of the gift of righteousness will reign in life through the One, Jesus Christ.*
>
> (Rom. 5:17)

This verse contrasts the power which resulted from Adam's sin with the grace available through Jesus Christ. Paul tells us that if we receive that which flows from Jesus, we will reign in life.

So what do we have to do? Paul wrote that we must *"receive the abundance of grace and of the gift of righteousness."* Let's tear into that statement. Let's see what treasure and revelation is buried here.

The first word we need to examine is "receive." Discovering the meaning of this word has been a step-by-step process for me. I had to go through a dramatic change before I even could begin understanding and applying this principle of receiving.

A major revelation concerning this came when my wife and I first began pastoring the church of which I spoke earlier. We were sent by an established denomination. A leader from headquarters arranged for us to take over a small congregation which had been meeting in a rented facility. As I mentioned, everything was a challenge when we first began to pastor.

In those early days, there was a lot of stress on both my wife and me. We were young, having been married only two years. Our first son had just been born prematurely. Not only were we left with the responsibility of a church and a new baby, but also with large medical bills.

The church offered numerous battles; the most pressing had to do with individuals and their struggles with personal sins. Alcohol, marijuana, and other drug use was common. Sexually perverse activities were reoccurring. In those early days, three people committed suicide. Others attempted it. Most of the congregation were older than I. Many had been married more than once. Some unmarried couples just were living together. Until being thrown into this environment, I didn't know people had such complicated and troubled lives.

I listened to their problems and did the best I could to offer counsel. The truth was, however, that I was in way over my head. I knew the Scriptures, but I had little to offer in application. I had lived a very sheltered life—for which I am grateful—but I did not have anywhere near the life-experiences which this group had.

Shortly after we took on the oversight of the church, the small congregation was on the verge of a split. Half the people were conservative and the rest had beliefs spanning the spectrum. The division broadened and then broke into outright war. Finally, the conservative, more stable side—those with good jobs—left. In addition, the denomination which had sent us to pastor decided they would no longer be our denominational covering. I was left with no building, no home, no oversight, little finances, and a small group of people with a lot of problems.

As we continued holding services in another building, I stood before the remaining congregation and gave my best. I met with people regularly and tried to demonstrate Christian strength and leadership. With tendencies toward perfectionism, I attempted to show my best side, but it was not enough.

There were times when I would be so exhausted and broken that I would go into the basement of our home, turn out the lights, lay on the couch, and cry. I had no strength left. I had no answers to give the people. Back in seminary, no one taught me how to deal with the situations I was facing. No one had told me ministry could be like this. I knew I did not have what these people needed. I cared for them, but I could not help. I was so exhausted and tormented at times that I did not want to face another day.

One time while I was crying on that couch, I dared something new. I had no strength...no energy to pray...no spiritual strength to rise up, nor even to read the Bible. With nothing to give to God, I whispered to Him, "Will You minister to me?"

Lying there in the dark, with tears welling up in my eyes, something began to flow from the Almighty. His love, His grace, His compassion—something of His nature—began to trickle down from heaven and nourish my soul. It warmed me. Substance from His nature reached into the depth of my heart and God ministered to me.

I always wanted to be strong. I thought I should be the mighty man of God who could use the Word of God and win any battle. I wanted to be the victorious soldier. I wanted to prove myself to God, worship Him constantly, give to Him. But that day, I could not give Him anything. I had nothing to offer. So I let God minister to me.

Something changed in my relationship with God that day. He became the Giver and I became the receiver. I let God bless me. I let Him love me. Since then, several times I have found myself unable to serve Him, worship Him, or give to Him. Yet, He always has been willing to give to me. Today, this is at the very foundation of my relationship with Him. He is the Giver and I am the receiver.

I think trees are smarter than people. Trees stand erect, spreading out their branches, allowing the sun and rain to bathe them. They do not strive to produce fruit, yet fruit comes forth. The more sun, nutrients, and water they receive, the more fruit they produce. Trees know how to receive. And in that receiving, they declare to man the relationship God maintains with all of His creation.

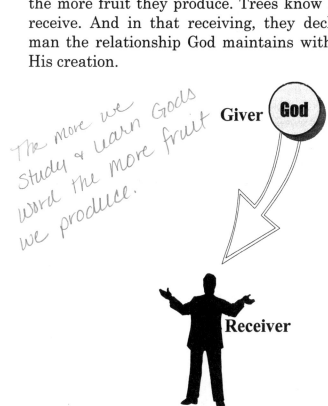

The more we study & learn Gods word the more fruit we produce.

Giver **God**

Receiver

James 1:17 tells us:

Every good thing bestowed and every
perfect gift is from above, coming
down from the Father of lights,....

Flowing from heaven is goodness, greatness, love, and everything that is wonderful. God is the *Source of all good things.*

Think this as you read Romans, chapter five. Pay special attention to our key verse, 5:17, where we are told to "receive the abundance of grace." See yourself standing beneath a river which flows from God and bathes over you. Grace is flowing into your being right now.

What is grace?

Most Christians confuse grace and mercy. In fact, some foreign languages make absolutely no distinction between these words. How tragic! Mercy and grace are very different.

To clarify this distinction, let's relate it to a real-life situation. In most countries speed limits are enforced by police officers. In our country, if you drive too fast, a police officer may chase you in his car with his lights flashing until you stop your automobile. After you pull over, the officer will drive behind you, walk up to your vehicle, and talk to you. If you are fortunate, he just will give you a warning and tell you to slow down, but if he decides to do so, he will give you a citation, which may cost you a significant sum of money.

Now, imagine the following scenario: a police officer pulls you over for speeding, walks up to your car, and talks to you. If he gives you a warning without a ticket, then you just received mercy. That is, you were forgiven and you did not receive the punishment due you. However, that is not grace. If the police officer gave you the warning and then, instead of handing you a ticket he gave you a gift of one thousand dollars (which I never have heard of a police officer doing), then you just received grace.

Do you see the difference between mercy and grace? Mercy is when you do not receive the *punishment which you deserve*. Grace is when you receive a *benefit which you do not deserve*.

All Christians understand mercy. They realize that they have been forgiven of their sins and, therefore, will not receive the punishment due them. However, most Christians do not understand grace, that it is different than mercy.

Mercy is good, but grace is wonderful, glorious, and powerful!

Not understanding this, many Christians continue to live under the power of sin and death, while pleading for God's mercy. Of course, God forgives them for their sins because He is a merciful God. Indeed, they are Christians because they believe in Jesus for the forgiveness of their sins. However, the Christian who only accesses the *mercy* of God will remain under the forces which push him to sin—forgiven, but still enslaved.

In Romans 5:17 we are instructed to receive an "abundance of grace." It is not enough to receive mercy. It is not enough to believe that your sins are forgiven. You must posture yourself under God's blessings which constantly flow from heaven. You must stand under that flow. You must receive it into your very nature. Only then will you reign in life.

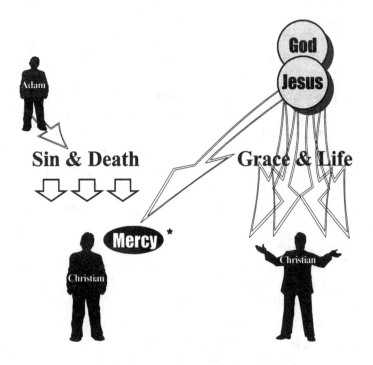

* In order to contrast grace and mercy, I have pictured them on separate sides of this diagram, but realize that even the Christian standing under grace will continue to need God's mercy.

Picture grace as a bucketful of liquid above your head. This liquid is pouring out for you to drink into your heart, soul, and whole nature. Now see a BIG bucket. Not a one-gallon bucket...not a five-gallon bucket...but a bucket bigger than your car, bigger than your house, bigger than the largest building you know. That bucket of grace is pouring out right above your head at this very instant. It is God's favor, power, and nature being poured out on your behalf.

If you want to reign in life, you must receive an "abundance" of this grace. Be thirsty, needy, desirous, even greedy for God's nature to flow into you right now. It is available—free and abundant. There is a waterfall of grace right over your head now. Receive.

He Will Cause You to Obey

5

There is a promise toward the end of Romans chapter five, which sounds almost too good to be true. Paul writes:

> *For as through one man's disobedience the many were made sinners, even so through the obedience of the One the many will be made righteous.* (Rom. 5:19)

Think about this. When Adam sinned, a power was released which activated a force pushing people to sin. That force works on every human being, enslaving them to the power of sin. In a comparable fashion, there is a force—grace—which flows from Jesus Christ. That force of grace makes us righteous.

The righteousness of which is spoken here is not just the gift wherein God sees us as forgiven, and therefore, righteous. This power is contrasted to the power of sin which flows through Adam. As the power of sin *pushes* us to sin, there is another power available through Jesus Christ which *pushes* us to obey. We actually can have working in our life a power which helps us and even pushes us to do God's will.

I need that in my life. You need it in your life. We need a push to fulfill God's will.

Do you hear what Paul is teaching us? There is a power available to you and me that not only will allow us to reign in life, but also will cause us to obey God.

This is the fulfillment of God's promise in the Old Testament:

> *And I will put My Spirit within you and cause you to walk in My statutes, and you will be careful to observe My ordinances.* (Ez. 36:27)

Notice that God said His Spirit would "cause" us to obey Him.

God is pouring out His Spirit upon us. It comes by grace. That grace flows and causes us to obey God.

Some readers may want me to refrain from stating this so boldly. They would rather I taught that grace simply *helps* or *stimulates* us to obey. However, those terms are too weak. They do not fully state the truth. God gave us a promise to put His Spirit in us which will *cause* us to obey.

In fact, Paul put it in even stronger terms. Adam's sin makes us sin, and our Lord's obedience makes us obey. Two thousand years ago when Jesus said, "No," to sin, He was resisting sin for us. He was tempted in all ways, yet without sin. As He was obeying the Father, He was overcoming temptations for you and me.

Furthermore, as He overcame all sin and death through His life and resurrection, He was winning the battle for us. Now that we have the victorious Lord living within us, His victory and His obedience can be our victory and obedience.

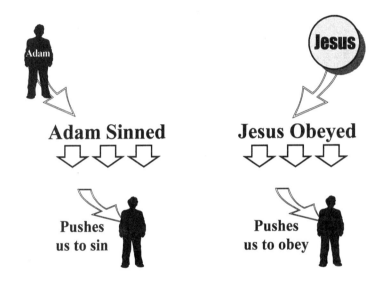

Adam Sinned

Pushes us to sin

Jesus Obeyed

Pushes us to obey

How are we to understand this "force of obedience"? If we search the Scriptures we find God working in the lives of individuals with different levels of this "grace-force." At one extreme we can see God pursuing Jonah until he finally fulfilled God's command to go preach in the city of Nineveh. God was even more forceful as He dealt with Saul on the road to Damascus, striking Saul down with a bright light, blinding his eyes, and speaking from heaven (Acts 9:1-19). God can and does (at times) work that forcefully, but He also works in a gentler fashion. Paul told us how he worked with the grace and power of God:

> ...*I labor, striving according to His power, which mightily works within me.* (Col. 1:29)

Paul had to cooperate and even exert effort to work with God. However, we cannot miss the underlying truth that God was supplying a power so that Paul could fulfill God's will.

God works this way in our lives. Paul wrote to the Philippian Christians:

> *for it is God who is at work in you, both to will and to work for His good pleasure.* (Phil. 2:13)

Here is good news: God is at work in you—inspiring, guiding, stimulating, compelling, and causing you to obey Him. Further, He is deepening within you the desire to do His will.

There is a power available to you and me. Just as there is a law of sin and death which acts as the law of gravity, forcing people down, so also there is a law of life in Christ Jesus which raises us to new levels of godliness. Yes, there is a force of grace which will help us to obey.

GOD GETS
ME OUT OF BED

6

Allow me to give you a personal testimony of how grace pushed me to obey in a very simple area of my life.

There was a time when I realized that I had drifted away from personal prayer and devotions with the Lord. I was becoming more and more aware of this lack in my life and I wanted to correct it. I wanted to arise early in the morning and dedicate an hour to quiet meditation and the study of God's Word. However, I found myself unable to get out of bed. Instead, I would lie there thinking I should get up, feeling bad that I was not praying, but still too tired to arise.

Grace lifted me. Instead of continuing to feel bad and trying to force myself up each morning, I decided to start receiving grace. For several mornings in a row I laid in bed, allowing God's grace to flow over me. I received it; I bathed in it. After about five days, I found the energy to get out of bed. In fact, I started eagerly looking forward to getting up early.

This may sound too good to be true, but I do not know how to explain the power of grace better than to flat out tell you how it has worked in my own life. Grace *causes me to obey.*

Some readers may have a hard time believing this because they never have experienced the power of grace in this fashion. All Christians have learned how our salvation is given to us by grace. But many never have understood how power over sin also is given to us by grace.

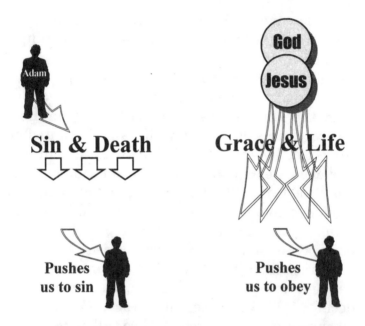

Indeed, trees are smarter than people. Trees receive. They yield to the energy and strength which comes from above. People just can't seem to realize that this is the answer. He who has an ear to hear, let him hear: the victory and obedience of Jesus is available to you and me. There is an overcoming power available to us. We must receive it.

Many Christians define "grace" as "God's unmerited favor." In accepting this "weak" definition, they envision God in heaven forgiving their sins and smiling down on them, even though they may not deserve it. In reality, grace is much more than God's forgiveness or smile.

It is true that God's grace is undeserved. However, the grace which flows from heaven toward you and me is *active*. It works in and for us. It causes us to obey. It changes us. Grace transforms our very nature into the nature of God.

The writer of the book of Hebrews explained:

> ...*it is good for the heart to be strengthened by grace, not by foods....*   (Heb. 13:9)

Grace will strengthen you. Just as food can be consumed and ingested, so also grace can be drawn into your being to increase your strength.

In the book of Romans, as Paul was contrasting the force released through Adam with the force released through Jesus Christ, he repeatedly stated and implied that the power of grace is *much greater* than the power of sin and death (i.e., Rom. 5:17; 8:2). To understand this *much greater power*, we must see it as actually flowing from heaven, entering our very nature, and transforming us. Grace is active power!

This grace is not just a one-time gift which we receive when we first become a Christian. Of course, we became Christians by the initial receiving of grace, but Paul is teaching us in Romans five through eight how to *live in this grace*. Grace is a mighty river constantly flowing from heaven, available to you and me on an ongoing, minute-by-minute basis.

Christians have not been forgiven of sins, saved from the coming judgment, and then left to be beaten down by the power of sin all the days of their lives. There is a power available to us right now which can set us free of the power of sin and death. It will cause us to *reign* in life (Rom. 5:17). Instead of sin reigning over us, grace will cause us to reign over sin.

Toward the end of Romans, chapter five, Paul offered us further good news when he said:

> ...where sin increased, grace abounded all the more....
> (Rom. 5:20)

Paul was speaking of God's provision in the midst of personal temptations and trials. When they increase, so does God's grace.

Think about this. The moment you are tempted to lose your temper, yield to lustful desires, say something that hurts another person, give up faith, or fall to some other sin, that is the moment when God's grace is being poured out most abundantly on your behalf. The bigger the temptation, the bigger the river of grace pouring out over your head.

Some of my readers may be crying out at this point, saying, "How?" In the pages to follow I will answer that in a step-by-step fashion so you will not misunderstand the profound truths Paul was laying out for us in Romans five through eight.

I'M DEAD TO SIN

You either are living under the power of sin and death or living under grace and life. Sin can reign over you or you can reign in life. This is what Paul taught in Romans chapter five.

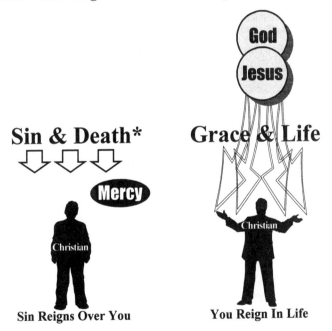

---

* In the diagram above, I am not showing Adam as the channel of sin and death. We know that sin entered into the world through him, yet sin and death continue to be active throughout the world because all people sin. Our sins influence the people around us. Therefore, we all share in the responsibility now.

Beginning in chapter six, Paul explained how we can move from under sin and death, and then into and under grace. Paul compares this move with water baptism (Rom. 6:3-5). As we go under water, it represents our burial with Christ in His death. As we come out of the water, we are united with Him in His resurrection. In giving us this analogy, Paul wants us to understand water baptism, but also the transition we should make from the old life to the new.

Think about the two stages separately: the death of Jesus and the resurrection. We identify with both events in water baptism.

Consider the death aspect. This death does not refer to the time when our heart stops beating and we quit breathing. Rather, Paul is referring to dying to the old nature and the past way of living, that is, the nature and lifestyle which an individual experienced while under the power of sin and death.

This death, which is represented by going under water in baptism, is a past-tense act. By this we mean that we should think and act as if we have already died with Jesus. In chapter six, each time Paul refers to our death, he uses terms which indicate that it is an accomplished fact:

...we have been buried with Him....
(6:4)

...we have become united with Him in the likeness of His death.... (6:5)

...our old self was crucified.... (6:6)

Some Bible translations do not emphasize this; however, it is important for you to know that the Greek language, from which our Bibles were translated, makes it very clear that the death of our old self is something we should consider done and completed in the past.

When speaking of the old life, Paul never tells us to die or cause our own death. Instead, he exhorts us to *consider it a finished work.* For example, chapter six, verse 11 tells us:

> *Even so consider yourselves to be dead to sin....*

The King James version of this verse uses the word, *reckon*, that is, we are exhorted to reckon ourselves dead to sin. Paul does not tell us to kill ourselves, put ourselves to death, or in any way act negatively toward our old nature. Our job is to *consider* the old man dead.

This concept is foreign to many Christians. They have been taught wrongly that they are to spend their lives crucifying the flesh and putting to death the evil within them. For those who have been indoctrinated into that way of thinking, it may be difficult to understand what I am explaining here. At this point I must ask for your patience as I continue to develop Paul's teaching on how we are to deal with the old man. I promise you, by the time you are done reading this book, you will see the path to the victorious Christian life through different eyes. For now, I must ask that you simply believe Paul's words. Our job is *to consider ourselves dead*, that is, to identify ourselves with the death of Jesus Christ which happened 2,000 years ago.

As long as Christians think of their old nature as still alive, they never will be able to escape the power of sin. If they still are fighting or trying to crucify the flesh, they still are considering their flesh alive.

This is where many Christians fail. For example, when an individual has negative thoughts come into his mind, he can either engage in a war to fight those thoughts or simply realize that those thoughts are not his. He does not have to take ownership of those thoughts because his old nature is dead. Instead, he can rejoice in the freedom of grace.

This is the first step in moving from under the power of sin and death. If a person *reckons* himself as dead, just as Paul exhorts us, he will be free to move under grace.

I'M ALIVE UNTO GOD **9**

Water baptism is a picture of how we move from under the power of sin into the new lifestyle under grace. Paul explained how going under the water portrays our identification with the death of Jesus. Now let's see how coming out of the water portrays our identification with His resurrection.

Paul wrote:

> *For if we have become united with Him in the likeness of His death, certainly we shall be also in the likeness of His resurrection.*
>
> (Rom. 6:5)

Notice the two stages. First, we are united with our Lord in His death, and second, we are united with Him in His resurrection.

We are to identify with our Lord's resurrection. Paul exhorts us:

> *Even so consider yourselves to be dead to sin, but alive to God in Christ Jesus.*   (Rom. 6:11)

Our job is to "consider," or as the King James version says, "reckon yourselves alive unto God."

We need to come to a clear revelation of this truth—enough to say, "I am alive!"

As we reckon ourselves alive, the life of God flows into our very nature. This is not just a one-time event. Nor is it something which will only take place after we get to heaven. The life of which Paul is speaking is the ongoing flow of life from God through Jesus Christ. It is available to you and me every minute of every day.

Embrace the whole picture Paul is developing for us. The power of sin and death came into the world through Adam and now is active throughout mankind. Through Jesus Christ there is released a much greater power—grace and life. As Christians, we can escape the first power and enter into the second.

Sin & Death

Grace & Life

God

Jesus

Consider Yourself Dead To Sin

Christian

Christian

Consider Yourself Alive Unto God

The old man living under the power of sin and death.

The new man living under grace and life.

Just as sin and death worked in us when we were under Adam, so grace and life will work in us as we move under Jesus Christ. In fact, it is the resurrection life of Jesus which will flow into our very nature.

Our part is to "consider." The only two things Paul thus far has told us to do is consider ourselves dead to sin but alive to God.

Just as Paul exhorted us to consider ourselves dead to sin and alive to God, the third and final thing he tells us to do is "present" ourselves. He instructs us not to present ourselves to sin, but rather to God:

> ... *present yourselves to God as those alive from the dead, and your members as instruments of righteousness.*   (Rom. 6:13)

This "presenting" is not difficult. Many Christians make the victorious life too hard, when God never meant it to be. God has made provisions for us to reign.

Present yourself to Him. See yourself standing under the abundant flow of His grace. Say to God, "Here I am." Open your arms wide and receive all that He has for you. Let God bless you. Let Him love you. Let God pour His nature and power into your very being.

A powerful picture of this posture before God is in the Old Testament where the high priest presented himself to be consecrated and ordained (Ex. 29:20-25). First, the priest was consecrated to God as blood from the sacrifice was rubbed on his body and then sprinkled over his garments.

Note how this parallels the New Testament understanding of how the blood of Jesus cleanses us from all sin (I John 1:7). Then anointing oil, representing the Holy Spirit, was sprinkled over the high priest. Finally, the other priests would place the fat cuts of the sacrifice and the bread which had been standing in the presence of the Lord into the hands of the high priest. The best that could be given was placed in his open arms as he stood before God. This is how the priest was ordained for God's work.

Present yourself in this fashion before God. Receive the abundance. Receive the best He has to offer. He wants to pour the nature of His own Son, the Lamb of God, into your nature.

Three things Paul has taught us to do:

1. Consider ourselves dead to sin
2. Consider ourselves alive unto God
3. Present our members alive unto God

As we do these three things, we will find ourselves standing under the abundant flow of grace. It is in that place where we can live in power and reign in life. And it is easier than you may think.

FREED FROM SIN!

11

Have you ever wished God just would take over and direct your life? Have you ever prayed, "God take me, possess me, make me yours!"? Well, God wants to answer that prayer. In Romans, chapter six, Paul explains the benefits of living under grace. He explained that if we do the things which we discussed in the preceding pages, then we shall live victoriously. Further, Paul writes:

...for he who has died is freed from sin. (Rom 6:7)

Do you want to be freed from sin? Of course, you do. Well, Paul tells us that it is possible! His words are not just idealistic hopes that vanish as we try to grasp them. Paul is talking about real benefits which we can have in our lives.

When we step out from under the power of sin and death, we become freed of the negative, evil forces. When we move under the grace of God, we step into a positive force which will push us in the direction of obedience.

...and having been freed from sin, you become slaves of righteousness. (Rom. 6:18)

Yes, there is a power available to you and me which will cause us, motivate us, push us, and even enslave us to act righteously.

Do you want His help in becoming good? Here is how to get it. Step into the flow of grace. Open your arms like the high priest and receive God's best.

Consider the consequences of living under this grace. Paul tells us:

> *But now having been freed from sin and enslaved to God, you derive your benefit, resulting in sanctification....*
> (Rom. 6:22)

"Freed from sin!" "Enslaved to God!" "Sanctification?" Can this be possible? Yes!

Sanctification means "set apart" and "made holy for God." That is the benefit, the result, the consequence which you and I will see in our lives as we learn to live under grace.

Brothers and sisters, there is no other path to the victorious Christian life while you are alive on planet earth. This is it. This is what Paul was trying to get us to understand. If you come to embrace this lifestyle, you will discover a new way of living which will set you free from sin and make you holy.

Now Live Under Grace

12

Several years ago I spent an extended period studying Romans five through eight in an effort to understand "living under grace." I was praying to God, asking Him to help me understand and live victoriously. Most of my earnestness to understand this area was due to my own personal struggles. I especially was trying to conquer thoughts which were not glorifying to God. I knew there had to be a way to escape and overcome, so I earnestly sought answers.

One day as I was driving my car on a long trip, a vision came to me that brought some things to light. It was God answering my prayers in picture form.

In the vision, a woman was talking to her pet bird. This woman, whom I will call Clare, loved her bird and every day she would sit for a while, drink tea, and visit with her pet. The bird would happily sing in response to Clare's affection.

One day as Clare was leaving for work, she saw that it was beautiful outside, so she took her bird in its cage and set it out on the porch. The bird was happy in the sunlight, so Clare left it out while she went to work. When she came home, Clare could see that her bird liked the fresh evening air, so she left it out for the whole night. When morning came she went out for her cup of tea with her beloved companion. Everything went so well that she decided to leave her bird outside for another day.

Day after day, this arrangement continued to work wonderfully, and the bird grew comfortable with his fresh-air surroundings.

Three months passed and the evenings began to cool as winter settled in. But Clare did not realize that it was getting too cold for her bird to remain outside. Then one day as she was visiting with her bird, she noticed that it was no longer singing. In a couple more days it was sick, huddled in a fluffy little ball trying to stay warm. Clare did not know why her bird was ill. She simply overlooked how the days had turned cooler.

After a week of seeing her bird getting weaker, she called the veterinarian, who recommended some medicine. Unfortunately, the veterinarian never was told that the bird had been living out in the cold.

Clare faithfully gave her bird the medicine four times each day. With a tiny eyedropper, she forced the bird to take in several drops of the liquid that was suppose to help. But things just got worse and worse, until the bird was lying at the bottom of its cage, trembling and unable to move. Reluctantly Clare went off to work that day thinking her bird might not live.

Later as she was driving home, anxious and fearful, the weather turned worse and it started to snow. Then the light went on. Seeing the snow falling around her house, she suddenly realized that her bird must be cold!

Clare hurried out of her car and ran to the house. She grabbed the cage where the weak little creature was barely breathing. Apologizing profusely, she placed the bird and its cage in the warmest location in the house. Then she settled down for the night, hoping her bird would live.

In the morning, the bird was sitting upright, not completely healed, but looking better. Happy and hopeful, Clare went off to work. When she returned, her bird was sitting on its perch looking around the room. The next morning she awoke to hear a few chirps. In just a few more days the bird was singing and acting normal, full of life.

This is where my vision ended.

Understanding came later. You and I are like that little bird. We get sick—spiritually—when we live in the wrong environment. When we realize that we are weak, unable to resist sin, we try medicine. Our medicine may be to run to church, read the Bible more, try to appease God, or simply pray. All of those things have benefit, but none of them will heal us. What we need is a different environment. We need to get under the love, power, acceptance, and warmth of God. Ultimately, only in the place of grace can we become healthy.

If we come into that place of grace, we will, indeed, become healthy. A healthy bird does not have to strive to sing or please its owner. If it is healthy, these things come naturally. So also a child of God will please God if he is healthy. It comes by nature—the new nature which God has instilled within him and now breathes to life.

GOD AT
WORK IN ME

13

In the Introduction of this book, I told you that no teaching has changed my life so profoundly as this one. That is true, however, I do not want to make this seem like some magical cure-all which completely and instantly fixes everything. I have faced trials and struggled with problems in my own life, and even today I am far from perfect. However, I have discovered how grace empowers me to get through trials and be more victorious. I have been so impacted by grace that I need to share it with everyone I meet. I want you to understand the transforming, resurrection power of grace.

I spent years struggling with depression and suicidal tendencies. I wondered if God ever would set me free. Even though I was in ministry, constantly speaking to people about our Lord Jesus, I quietly battled with tormenting thoughts. At times I would condemn myself for living such a defeated, helpless lifestyle. Other times I would force myself to action in spite of the forces pushing me to give up. I couldn't control my thoughts and I hated myself for it. Sometimes I would be angry at God for not caring enough to deliver me. After more than 12 years of living confused and tormented, I gave up hope of ever getting free.

Then I discovered grace. I had known the grace of my initial salvation for years. However, when I learned that grace was pouring from heaven 24 hours of every day, I began to let God bless me.

The first significant step to victory was when God brought a special couple into my life to pray for me. They had faith to set people free. Indeed, after an evening of ministry by them, I no longer had to battle with thoughts of such hopelessness that I wanted to end my life.

However, I still suffered with less severe depression. At times my thoughts were far from glorifying to God.

As I continued learning about grace and trying to live under its flow, I found myself guided down a new path. I began living differently. Instead of constantly forcing myself to produce in my daily life, I relaxed more. This was not an instantaneous change; it took awhile.

Gradually, I came to understand God differently. I became comfortable with God being the Giver in our relationship. Grace allowed me to escape a lifestyle of stress, thinking I must force myself to win God's approval. I learned how to sit quietly, doing absolutely nothing except letting God's grace pour into my being.

As my lifestyle changed, I stopped pushing myself to exhaustion. Later I learned that many of my problems were the result of years of self-imposed stress. When a person keeps himself constantly under pressure, he depletes himself of certain chemicals in his nervous system which are necessary for healthy thought patterns. Most of my tormenting thoughts were the consequences of my lifestyle, therefore, the long-term solution was not to control my thoughts, but to change my lifestyle. I became less of a perfectionist. The more I began living as God wanted me to live, the more I was able to have a healthier thought life.

I also learned my limits. I established boundaries in my life so I would not get exhausted. This involved not letting people take advantage of me nor demand so much from me that I later would be unable to function. In other words, I learned how to say, "No." I also limited ministry time and began enjoying a hobby, which for me was working on wood projects.

My deliverance did not stop there. The grace of God led me down a path to freedom. It was as if I were guided to talk to the right people at the right time and read the books I needed as I was able to receive them. My diet also changed. I stopped drinking so much coffee. I started to exercise. I drank more water. I even found help in medical treatment for a time.

None of these steps seemed particularly difficult at the time. God just seemed to lead me one step at time into a more healthy lifestyle.

During that transition of life, my relationships with people also changed. My marriage became more relaxed and blessed. My wife and I became more one in heart. I began enjoying my children more, learning how to laugh with them. I developed deeper friendships. I stopped being so anti-social—a major change for me.

Today, I realize that God was not interested in me just overcoming bad thoughts. He wanted to heal my whole life. He wanted a different type of relationship with me. Once I began living in grace, God began orchestrating my life, bringing the right people, circumstances, information, and help into my life. I changed. As a consequence, my thought patterns became more and more glorifying to Him.

Grace is a *pathway to freedom*. As a person learns to live under grace, they learn a new way of living. That new lifestyle carries them down a road to freedom.

Your path to freedom will be different than mine. You may discover completely different steps toward the goal of living victoriously. However, receiving grace puts you on that path.

The most important truth I hope to impart is that "God is at work." Paul reassured us:

> *...He who began a good work in you*
> *will perfect it....*   (Phil. 1:6)

God is not unconcerned about our struggles and trials. Rather, He is willing and active in bringing us into the victorious life. Paul tells us:

> *...we are His workmanship, created*
> *in Christ Jesus for good works....*
>   (Eph. 2:10)

We have a tendency to want to perfect ourselves. Yet it is God's job to change us.

In the Old Testament, God declared that He is the Lord who sanctifies us (Ez. 20:12). He is the One who makes us holy. This holiness is not imaginary, nor is it only a cloak to cover our sins. It is more. God literally declares Himself to be the One who makes us holy. Yes, He will cause us to obey!

In my own life, I repeatedly have seen the reality to this. In addition to depression, I have wrestled with other trials and temptations. I have passions the same as any man. At times, receiving grace has given me instant freedom. Other times, it puts me on the road to freedom. Either way, I am convinced—grace works.

Although I personally never struggled with alcohol, drug use, or other addictive substances, I know and have worked with people who have been set free. Some discovered grace and instantly they were delivered from all desires for the addictive substance. Others found freedom in a step-by-step fashion. As they learned to receive grace—the active, transforming, resurrection power of God—doors opened before them. As they walked through those doors, they received the help that was offered. As they opened to a lifestyle of letting God pour out His grace on their behalf, they discovered a power which was guiding them. They found themselves being led down a path to freedom.

Once I was blind, but now I see. I am not perfect, but nor am I tormented anymore. There is a power flowing from heaven toward me. It bathes me. It protects me. It transforms me. It resurrects me into the victory of Jesus Christ. It continues to lead me into greater and greater freedom.

GOD
GAVE THE LAW

14

Now it is time to understand the place of the Law. Throughout Romans, the apostle Paul refers to the Law which God gave through Moses to the Jewish people. Understanding the proper place of the Law is of great benefit for the Christian learning how to live under grace.

In Old Testament times, all people were living under the influence of sin and death. Jesus had not yet come to provide forgiveness of sins nor to release the fullness of grace. However, God loved the people and He reached out to them. Through Moses, God gave the Law and He established a covenant with the Jews.

The Law was a blessing from God. It was the means by which God revealed His will and established order for society. Through the Law God reached out to the Jewish people. The Law was a part of God's covenant through which He could communicate with, set apart, and bless the people who were obedient (Deut. 28).

The Law was good. However, it never freed people from the power of sin and death. God established a different avenue by which the people could be freed—Jesus Christ. Through Jesus there is an abundance of grace being poured out to free people from the power of sin and death.

The Apostle John contrasted what came through Moses with what came through Jesus:

For the Law was given through Moses; grace and truth were realized through Jesus Christ. (John 1:17)

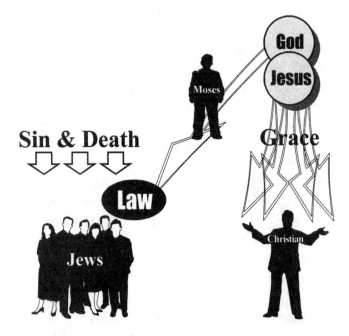

The Apostle Paul explained the function of the Law in Romans, chapters six and seven. This was of special interest to the Jews in Paul's day, but these truths are also essential for us (as we will see in the next chapters when we consider the laws under which we place ourselves).

THE LAW DOES NOT PRODUCE HOLINESS   **15**

Paul had a major job on his hands when he attempted to explain to the Jewish people that they need to live under grace rather than under the Law. They had centered their lives around the Law of God. They always had been taught the value of God's commandments, and they were earnest in trying to live accordingly.

Before Paul could show them a different way to live, he had to convince the Jews that the Law would not work. It could not make people holy.

Paul explained the negative effect of the Law. As people try to live up to the commandments of the Law, they find themselves unable to do so. In fact, they soon learn that knowledge of certain commandments actually stirs rebellion inside of them and leads to more sin:

> *But sin, taking opportunity through the commandment, produced in me coveting of every kind....when the commandment came, sin became alive....*   (Rom. 7:8-9)

This point is very important because the Jews of Paul's day thought that by following the Law they could become holy. In reality, the more people try abide by the standards of the Law, the more sin becomes activated in their lives.

As Paul explained this, he was careful to clarify that it is not the Law nor the commandments of God which make people sin. The Law is good. It is sin which dwells within us which is bad, and sin becomes more active as we try to live under the Law (Rom. 7:12-14).

To help the Jews break free of the Law, Paul used an analogy (Rom. 7:1-3). He wrote of a woman married to a man, and hence, under obligation to remain married to him. Only if the husband dies, Paul explained, is the wife free to marry another. In an analogous fashion, the Jews were married to the Law. However, now they needed to "die" to the Law, and hence, no longer live under that obligation. Once they were freed from the previous way of living, they would be free to live a new lifestyle, that is, under grace.

Consider again the fact that people who are under the Law are still under the power of sin and death. As we stated, the Law does not move people out from under the power of sin and death; it leaves them there. Therefore, if people want to escape from being under the power of sin and death, they also must get out from under the Law. This is why Paul was so intent on convincing the people that the Law never could set them free of sin or make them holy.

God has established a new way—the way of receiving grace through Jesus Christ. As long as people cling to the Law, they will hold themselves under and within the power of sin.

Now Fulfill
The Law

16

Today most Christians realize that they do not have to keep all of the Old Testament Laws; however, we have our own set of laws. Notice here I am not capitalizing the term *law*. I will use the capitalized term to refer to the Law which God gave to the Jewish people through Moses. When the term *law* is used, not capitalized, I am referring to rules and regulations which people develop and impose upon themselves and others. Every person develops his own laws, that is, standards by which he measures himself and others. For example, a person may have rules within his own mind such as, "Thou shalt not sleep in," "Thou shalt not smoke," or "Thou shalt not overeat," or "Thou shalt not have a bad thought." The list of self-imposed rules can be endless.

Placing ourselves under these laws is just as futile as the Jews placing themselves under the Laws given through Moses. Our natural man rebels to such laws and we find ourselves wanting to sin more.

Paul offers us the solution to this dilemma. He explains how the will of God will be fulfilled in us as we place ourselves under grace. He uses the term *law* in verse two of Romans eight, yet here he is referring to law in the sense of a force,

63

like the force of gravity. There is a law of life in Christ when we live under grace.

> *For the law of the Spirit of life in Christ Jesus has set you free from the law of sin and death.* (Rom. 8:2)

The law at work through Jesus is greater than the force at work through sin and death.

Sin & Death

Grace & Life

LAW OF SIN AND DEATH   LAW OF THE SPIRIT OF LIFE

We can make a comparison here with how the law of gravity is a force acting upon every person holding them down. However, when the wind catches the wings of an eagle, "lift" overcomes gravity, and the eagle flies. In similar fashion, the law of life in Christ overcomes and frees us from the law of sin and death.

Next Paul explains the results in the life of the person who lives under grace:

> *For what the Law could not do,*

weak as it was through the flesh, God did: sending His own Son...in order that the requirement of the Law might be fulfilled in us....

(Rom. 8:3-4)

When we are under grace, the law of life works in us, pushing us and moving us to obey God—then we fulfill the desires, will, and laws of God.

The laws we fulfill are not merely the Old Testament Laws. It is more than that. Jesus fulfilled the Mosaic Law, but He also fulfilled the perfect will of the Father. As He works within us, we ultimately fulfill the "highest law," which Jesus explained is to love the Lord our God with our whole heart and love our neighbor as ourselves (Matt. 22:37-39).

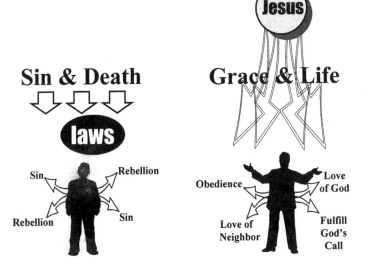

When a Christian lives under grace, he discovers power which enables and causes him to fulfill God's will. As Paul wrote in Philippians:

...for it is God who is at work in you, both to will and work for His good pleasure. (Phil. 2:13)

God is active within the Christian, causing him to do His will.

As a consequence, rules and regulations will not be a burden, and if they are according to God's will, they will be fulfilled.

Unhealthy "rules," those developed by guilt, compulsion, habit, or wrong teaching, will slip away. This is an important point, because many Christians are trying to force themselves to do things which God never wanted them to do. This is just as much bondage as living in sin. As a person learns to live under grace he discovers what truly is God's will. Some people's previously held laws dissolve in importance as God manifests His will in their lives.

This is good news!

Christians who find it difficult to do God's will still are living under the power of sin and death. They are not receiving enough of the grace which is offered to them. Once we access and live in the power of God, we find it possible—even natural—to do God's will.

It is worth adding here that the Law (or law) still has a place in the lives of people who refuse

God's grace. Paul explained:

> *But we know that the Law is good, if*
> *one uses it lawfully, realizing the*
> *fact that law is not made for a*
> *righteous man, but for those who are*
> *lawless and rebellious, for the*
> *ungodly and sinners, for the unholy*
> *and profane, for those who kill their*
> *fathers or mothers, for murderers*
> *and immoral men and homosexuals*
> *and kidnappers and liars and*
> *perjurers, and whatever else is*
> *contrary to sound teaching....*
> (I Tim. 1:8-10)

The Christian need not put himself under the law; however, the law still must be enforced in the lives of sinners. We still need police officers to enforce peace in society. We need teachers to maintain order in their classrooms. Rules and standards are good and must be enforced when necessary.

However, the Christian living under grace does not need enforcement of law to live a godly lifestyle. Grace will produce a much more holy and God-pleasing lifestyle than the enforcement of laws ever could.

As a friend of mine says: "Bridles are used to lead horses and leashes are for dogs; however, devoted pets follow at will."

During the Protestant Reformation of the Sixteenth Century, Martin Luther and other leaders boldly declared that we are saved by grace, not by works of the Law. This teaching has been a central theme of Protestants for the last 500 years. It is also one of Paul's major points in chapters three and four of Romans. The idea that we are saved by grace is foundational to the Christian faith.

However, in emphasizing grace as the door to salvation, Christians have tended to contrast grace and Law. Of course, salvation is available to us through grace, rather than the works of the Law; however, Christians have contrasted these two words, grace and Law, so much and for so many years, that they have consciously and subconsciously thought of them as opposites.

In reality, the terms grace and Law are not opposites.

To see this, consider how someone can associate and contrast two other words, even though they are not opposite in meaning. For example, someone may talk about cars and trucks. These are not opposites. In fact, both are beneficial, used for transportation purposes. Yet, in conversation a person may contrast the two with each other.

In an analogous way, we contrast the terms grace and Law, when we declare that people are saved by one, but not the other. Though this contrast is helpful, it does not mean that grace and Law are opposites.

The truth is that both grace and Law are good. Both came from God.

What, then, is the opposite of grace? The power of sin and death! One came through Jesus, the other came through Adam. One pushes us to sin. The other pushes us to obey. These are forces opposing one another. These are opposites.

Sin & Death ⟨Opposites⟩ Grace & Life

Unfortunately, many Christians are confused about this. When they wrongly think of grace and Law as opposites, they begin to think negatively of the Law (and laws). Knowing that grace is good, they tend to think of laws as bad. Therefore, they will consciously and subconsciously define grace as the *absence of laws.*

Consider the seriousness of this error. A Christian with this misunderstanding will say, "I am living under grace, not law!" In making this statement they are declaring that they will not subject themselves to any rules, and hence, they are not obligated to exercise self-discipline in any area of their life. In reality, that way of living does not lead to the victorious lifestyle, and it is completely foreign to what Paul was teaching.

Please realize that *living under grace has nothing to do with an absence of laws.* Again, I say that the opposite of grace is not law; the opposite of grace is the power of sin and death.

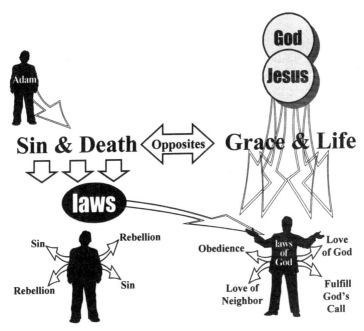

Living under grace changes the position of the law from over a person's head to within their heart. In addition, it activates the power of God to help them fulfill those laws.

Christians who understand this will say, "I am living under grace," and in making this statement they are declaring that they are living in the active power of God, which frees them from sin, causes them to obey God, and enables them to reign in life. This is very different than living in an absence of laws. The path to living the victorious Christian life is not a struggle to escape rules and regulations, but rather to move out from under the power of sin and death and into the power of God.

GET RID
OF CONDEMNATION

18

Once we see the place of the Law, we can understand Paul's powerful statement which begins chapter eight of Romans:

> *There is therefore now no condemnation for those who are in Christ Jesus.* (Rom. 8:1)

It is essential that Christians completely escape condemnation.

The truth is that we truly cannot get out from under the Law (or laws) as long as we are feeling condemned. In another passage, Paul tied the Law and condemnation together, referring to the "ministry of Law" as the "ministry of condemnation" (II Cor. 3:6-9). These two are inseparable, because the Law reveals to a person the will of God and, therefore, exposes areas in which they fall short. The ministry of the Law actually depends upon condemnation because it cannot be enforced without the pressure of condemnation.

The *power* of the Law is condemnation. This means that *guilt* is the Law's primary hold on people.

For example, as a person feels bad about himself, he forms thoughts in his mind, such as, "I am a bad person", "I need to try harder", "I need to control myself more," "I need to force myself to obey," etc. Such thoughts lead down a path to where the person is putting himself back under law.

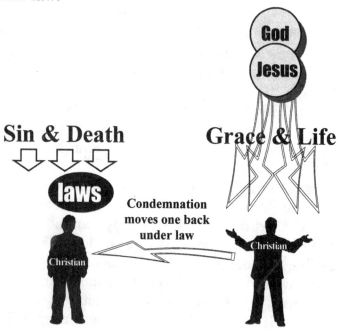

Tragically, the guilt-ridden person moves back under the power of sin and death. He cannot escape this. When a person moves back under law he puts himself under the negative forces which weaken him spiritually and make him sin.

The Christian who wants to live under grace must escape condemnation.

There are two types of condemnation: that which is associated with real sin and that which is simply a vague feeling of guilt.

Condemnation resulting from actual sins committed must be dealt with by confession to God. In I John 1:9, we are assured that:

If we confess our sins, He is faithful and righteous to forgive us our sins and to cleanse us from all unrighteousness.

The word *confess* means *to acknowledge* or *admit*. Hence, when we admit to God that we have committed certain sins, He not only forgives us, but also cleanses us of those sins.

We must believe this. If you have confessed a certain sin to God, then it is time for you to realize that God has forgiven and washed you of that sin.

People also suffer from a vague sense of not feeling right with God. They cannot think of anything they have done wrong, but they suspect that God dislikes them. Or they just don't quite know what He thinks, so they keep themselves under a little bit of self-condemnation, punishing themselves just in case they have done something bad.

I dare say, all Christians deal with this type of condemnation at times, and some Christians deal with it on a continual, ongoing basis.

We need to realize that any form of condemnation gives the Law (or law) power. We both consciously and subconsciously hold ourselves accountable, hold ourselves in check, and place subtle rules over our heads. Such thought patterns pull us back under the law which remains under the power of sin and death.

For this reason, Paul declares the good news: "there is therefore now no condemnation for those in Christ Jesus." None. Condemnation has been removed. Believe this. If you are aware of any specific sins, then confess them and accept God's forgiveness. If, on the other hand, you simply are keeping yourself under a little bit of condemnation, stop now. Don't live that way. It never will lead you into the victorious lifestyle.

God is not mad at you. We have peace with God through our Lord Jesus Christ (Rom. 5:1). Consider Paul's words later in Romans eight:

> *Who will bring a charge against God's elect? God is the one who justifies; who is the one who condemns? Christ Jesus is He who died....* (Rom. 8:33-34)

God is not condemning you. In fact, He is the One who went to great extents to provide forgiveness.

There is no condemnation coming from God. Don't put yourself under it. Move and stay under grace. Grace is free, undeserved power, leading to liberty, obedience, and holiness. Choose it.

THE BODY
OF DEATH

19

In chapter seven of Romans, Paul describes a struggle with which every Christian deals. Paul talks about the sin and rebellion which arises within us as we put ourselves under law, then he goes on to explain the battle between his inner man and outer man. He talks about wanting to do good on the inside, but finding sin and rebellion at work on the outside (Rom. 7:14-23).

It is important to identify where sin is at work. The Christian has had a change of heart and, therefore, wants to please God in the inner man. However, as Paul explains, the outer man is unwilling to obey.

It is the outer man which is subject to the law of sin and death. Paul explained:

> *For I joyfully concur with the law of God in the inner man, but I see a different law in the members of my body, waging war against the law of my mind, and making me a prisoner of the law of sin which is in my members.* (Rom. 7:22-23)

Notice where the forces of sin are at work—in the members of his body, that is, the outer man.

Sin & Death

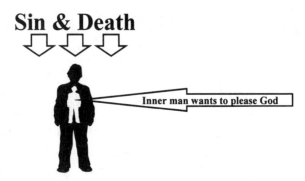

Inner man wants to please God

This struggle between the inner and the outer man creates a war. Unfortunately, the outer man often wins. It actually imprisons the inner man, making it impossible for a person to please God, as they really desire to on the inside.

Paul cries out the resulting anguish which so many Christians have experienced:

> *Wretched man that I am! Who will set me free from the body of this death?* (Rom. 7:24)

From what does he want to be freed? *The body of death*. Please remember that phrase as we go on to the solution. It is in our bodies that the power of sin and death is at work.

This is true even in the Christian's life. Paul made this clear in Romans eight, when he wrote:

> *If Christ is in you, though the body is dead because of sin, yet the spirit is alive because of righteousness.*
> (Rom. 8:10)

Notice Paul is talking about a Christian—someone who has Christ in them. He explains that their spirit has been made alive because of righteousness. However, the body is still dead. Not the type of death wherein a person would cease breathing and fall to the ground. But a body cut off from the life of God and, therefore, subject to the power of sin and death.

It is this *body of death* from which Paul cried out to be freed. This is our problem. How can we be freed from the body of death?

A Body
of Life

20

Paul ended chapter seven of Romans crying out to be delivered from his *body of death*. That body was a prison, restraining his inner man from obedience to God. Paul explained that as a Christian he could be both alive on the inside and dead on the outside. This created a war within and often left him defeated.

In chapter eight of Romans, Paul gives us the answer:

> *But if the Spirit of Him who raised Jesus from the dead dwells in you, He who raised Christ Jesus from the dead will also give life to your mortal bodies....*   (Rom. 8:11)

Notice the results of having the Spirit of God dwelling in us—God will give life to our mortal bodies.

This is the solution to Paul's cry, "Who will set me free from the body of this death?"

It is not enough just to have Jesus come and live in your spirit. Of course, that is how you become a Christian and, hence, have your spirit made alive unto God (Rom. 8:10). However, step two is to become filled with the Holy Spirit in such a way that your *body is resurrected to life.*

We are not talking about your body being resurrected after you die and are put into the grave. We are talking about the resurrection life of Jesus, available to you and me now, this day, this week, while we go through our daily routine. The same Spirit which resurrected Jesus from the grave 2,000 years ago will resurrect our bodies today.

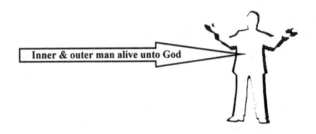

Inner & outer man alive unto God

When the body of the Christian is made alive and responsive to God, it is no longer subject to the power of sin and death. Then both the inner man and the outer man want to please God.

Many Christians never have understood this truth. They never have been taught that their outer man can be made alive unto God. They wrongly think that all the days of their lives they are to live with a battle raging between their inner man and outer man. They stay in chapter seven of Romans, crying out to God to be delivered from their bodies of death. No one has ever taught them how they also can have their bodies made alive unto God.

Grace is not only active power. It is resurrection power—transforming power—changing our bodies of death into bodies of life in Christ Jesus.

Sin & Death

A Christian whose outer man is conformed to the nature of Adam and the natural man.

Grace & Life

To receive grace is to receive the nature of Jesus. In contrast, a person who lives under the power of sin and death will have produced within him a sinful nature as Adam's fallen nature. The good news is this: a Christian can have his mortal body made alive unto God as the nature of Jesus manifests within him.

*...if the Spirit of Him who raised
Jesus from the dead dwells in you,
He...will also give life to your mortal
bodies....* (Rom. 8:11)

Your body—if it is spiritually dead right now—
can be raised to life. It can happen today, while
you are reading these words.

What is the requirement for this resurrection
of our bodies? The Spirit of Him who raised Jesus
from the dead must dwell in us. How can we have
the Spirit of God (that is, the Holy Spirit) dwell
in us in the way Paul is teaching? Let's find out.

Various Christian groups have their own
unique way of explaining what it means to have
the Holy Spirit dwell in them. Some talk about a
baptism of the Holy Spirit, others about an in-
filling of the Spirit, and others claim that
receiving the Spirit is synonymous with
becoming born again. Whatever your previous
training has been, please, try to look at this
through new eyes. Every person has a tendency
to read things through the training which they
already have received. I am concerned that many
may miss what Paul was trying to teach us
because they already have their minds pre-
programmed to one way of thinking.

See Roman 8:11 in its context. Throughout chapters five to eight, Paul developed a step-by-step explanation of how the Christian can escape the power of sin and death. Paul was giving us the answers to life's battle with sin. He was telling us how we can live under grace and reign in life.

Understand Romans, chapter eight with that picture in mind. Paul is not changing the subject. He is completing the picture by explaining the role of the Holy Spirit.

Therefore, we must not think of the Holy Spirit as separate from everything else we have learned. It is the Holy Spirit which Jesus received from the Father and now pours out upon us (Acts 2:33). To receive God's grace is to receive God's Spirit. The Holy Spirit is, in fact, the "Spirit of Grace" (Heb. 10:29).

Further, Paul exhorts us in Romans 8:4-5 to walk "according to the Spirit." This is contrasted with walking "according to the flesh." In reality, when we live under sin and death, we are walking according to the flesh. When we live under grace and life, we are walking according to the Spirit.

When Paul exhorts us to "walk according to the Spirit," he is not talking about a one-time experience of being filled or baptized in the Holy Spirit. He is talking about a lifestyle of living under grace—to walk in it. To be bathed in grace is to be bathed in the Holy Spirit. To be filled with this grace is to be filled with the Spirit.

Sin & Death
⇩ ⇩ ⇩

Sin · Rebellion

Rebellion · Sin

**A Christian walking
according to the flesh**

Love
Joy

Peace
Patience

Kindness
Goodness

Faithfulness
Self-control

**A Christian walking
according to the Spirit**

The victorious life is the outcome of culti-vating a lifestyle of constantly receiving God's abundant grace, which is being given to us by way of the Holy Spirit. Picture yourself walking around all week long, continually bathed in the grace, love, and power of God. Receive it! Allow it to flood into your being. Let Him bless you.

**BORN OF
FLESH OR SPIRIT?**   **22**

To continue our study of the victorious life, we need to explain what the "flesh" is and how to overcome it.

The term *flesh* is used with two different meanings in the Bible.

In the Old Testament times, the word referred to the skin, meat, and other tissues of animals and man. For example, the Jewish priests offered the *flesh* of animals on the altar (i.e., Deut. 12:27). This natural definition also is used in some places in the New Testament when speaking of the physical bodies of living things (i.e., Acts 2:31; Heb. 9:10). When speaking of the flesh in these contexts, flesh is neither good nor bad, but simply the physical part of a living creature.

However, our Lord Jesus brought new meaning to this term when He said:

> *"That which is born of the flesh is flesh, and that which is born of the Spirit is spirit."*   (John 3:6)

When Jesus referred to *flesh* here, He was not speaking of the meat tissue of living things. He was referring to flesh as *whatever has been born of man's sinful nature.*

In this context, flesh is bad.

Paul frequently used this definition of *flesh*. For example, in I Corinthians he told the Christians who were quarreling that they were "men of flesh" (3:1) and "fleshly" (3:3). In this context, the word *fleshly* can be interchanged with *carnal*.

In the book of Galatians, Paul lists the deeds of the flesh:

> *...immorality, impurity, sensuality, idolatry, sorcery, enmities, strife, jealousy, outbursts of anger, disputes, dissensions, factions, envying, drunkenness, carousing, and things like these....* (Gal. 5:19-21)

These are the deeds of man's sinful nature.

Flesh produces flesh. As man lives under and yields to the evil forces around him, he becomes fleshly. His sin nature grows. That nature then produces more fleshly thoughts and desires.

Sin & Death

Fleshly Thoughts

Carnal Ideas

Deeds of the Flesh

Fleshly Desires

In contrast, our Lord stated that whatever is born of Spirit is "spirit." As the Holy Spirit is allowed to work in our lives, the fruit of the Spirit is produced:

> *...love, joy, peace, patience, kindness, goodness, faithfulness, gentleness, self-control....*   (Gal. 5:22-23)

These things are set in contrast to the deeds of the flesh. They are spiritual and holy. They are "born" of the Holy Spirit.

Spiritual Thoughts

Good Deeds

Fruit of the Spirit

Holy Desires

Having defined these terms, we next need to see how we get free of the flesh, that is, free of the carnal, evil side of our being.

Many Christians have been taught wrongly that they never can get free of the flesh. Instead, they have been taught that the flesh will be resident in them for as long as they are alive on this earth. Of course, we will not get free of our physical bodies while we are alive on this earth. However, we can get free of the flesh if we are referring to the carnal nature within us.

This is what Paul taught us in Romans eight:

> *However, you are no longer in the flesh but in the Spirit, if indeed the Spirit of God dwells in you.*
>
> (Rom. 8:9)

Notice that it is possible to escape the flesh, that is, to "no longer be in the flesh."

I wish I could shout this phrase a thousand times to every Christian: "no longer in the flesh!" It is possible to be free of the flesh.

How is it possible? The flesh is not a fixed part of our being, nor forever resident within. Rather, it is whatever in our nature has been produced by the power of sin and death. Therefore, if we can get out from under the power of sin and death, we can escape the flesh. As the Spirit of God fills us, our fleshly thoughts turn into spiritual thoughts. Our carnal desires turn into holy desires. The deeds of the flesh diminish and the fruit of the Spirit manifests.

Think of the transformation this way. The fleshly part of our being is like ice on top of a glass of water. If the water is placed under the warm light, the ice will melt away. In similar fashion, the carnal nature is eliminated as we live under the grace, love, and power of God. On the other hand, if we go back to living under the power of sin and death (in the freezer), flesh (ice) will form again.

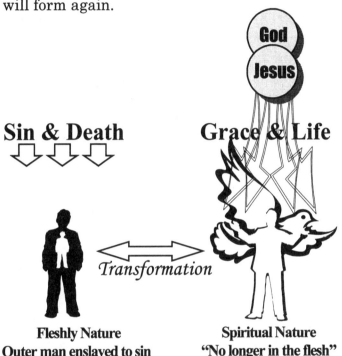

Sin & Death

Grace & Life

Transformation

Fleshly Nature
Outer man enslaved to sin

Spiritual Nature
"No longer in the flesh"

This understanding is key. Realizing that the flesh can be transformed makes it easy to see how we can live the victorious Christian life. Our job is not to fight the flesh. In fact, a Christian who is fighting the flesh does not yet understand what Paul was teaching about this subject. To fight the flesh means one is still "in the flesh." Paul was teaching us how to "no longer be in the flesh," and, in fact, free of it so, we do not have to fight with it.

93

As a mother gives birth to a baby, Spirit gives birth to spirit. Fleshly desires turn into holy desires. Fleshly thoughts turn into holy thoughts. This is what the Spirit does in us. He transforms our fleshly nature into a spiritual nature which wants to please God.

Of course, we are not saying that all of this is instantaneous. However, we are saying that this is the path to the victorious Christian life: not by fighting the flesh, but by living according to the Spirit.

THE LETTER KILLS; THE SPIRIT GIVES LIFE

The principles we have been studying in the book of Romans also were explained to the Christians who lived in Corinth. Paul wrote to them contrasting the ministry of the Law with the ministry of the Spirit. He told about the new covenant which we have with God, in which God pours out His grace by the Spirit, and, hence, we are transformed into the image of our Lord, from glory to glory (II Cor. 3:6-18).

In that passage, Paul explained that both the Law and grace are ministries of God, that is, they are ways in which God reached down to help mankind. In fact, both the Law and grace have glory; however, the ministry of grace has much greater glory (II Cor. 3:7-9).

Paul further explains that even though the Law is good, it cannot transform us. The Law comes with condemnation and it *kills*, that is, it decreases our spiritual life, vitality, and energy (II Cor. 3:6). If we try to live under the Law, we find ourselves weakened spiritually.

In contrast, "the Spirit gives life" (II Cor. 3:6). As we live within the new covenant of God, bathing in the grace which pours from heaven, spiritual energy and vitality arise from within us. Rivers of living water flow from our innermost being as we believe (John 7:38).

We all have experienced the effects of the law in our own lives. We can be under such heavy rules and expectations that we are overwhelmed. It can feel like a load too heavy to carry. Such legalism can crush us.

The laws which can overwhelm a person may be expectations to measure up to a high standard of performance. They may be a list of things that need to be accomplished when there is too little energy, help, provisions, or time. Unrealistic goals may become laws which kill spiritual strength.

These laws may be self-imposed or they may be placed upon us by another person. Our Lord Jesus rebuked the scribes and Pharisees who had so many rules for the common people that it was impossible for them ever to measure up (Matt. 23:4). This error most commonly is committed by individuals in leadership who have the authority to put expectations on people under their charge. Hence, a leader can be a minister of grace and life, or a minister of law and condemnation.

Though a ministry of condemnation kills spiritual vitality, it does have some glory (I Cor. 3:6-9). People can be intimidated and made to feel bad to such an extent that they may change their own behavior in minor ways. However, the ministry of grace and life has much greater glory, actually causing people to be transformed into the very image of God (II Cor. 3:9-18)

When one person condemns another it is often done unknowingly. For example, a certain minister simply may put a challenge on people to reach higher goals. If the minister is allowing the love and grace of God to flow through him, then there is little problem, and, in fact, challenges may be just what is needed. However, if condemnation flows along with the challenge, spiritual strength is diminished, and people may be crushed under the load.

What is legalism to one person may be grace and life to another. It always amazes me to hear the reactions of different people to a message given at a church. One listener may be challenged in a way that causes him to rise up and accomplish great things. Another person may be sitting in the same room, hearing the exact same message, but come out feeling spiritually beaten up.

Much depends upon a spiritual bond existing between the leader and the listener. If there is not a bond of love, it is easy for the listener to take the message as law and condemnation. (Similar dynamics can be set up between a husband and wife, between a parent and child, or within many other relationships.) The wise leader understands this and endeavors to reassure people of his love for them. He not only pretends to love, but he keeps his heart open and allows the grace of God flowing through his life and ministry.

It is the responsibility of every Christian to keep himself in the grace of God. Jude exhorts us to keep ourselves in the center of God's love (Jude 21). To do this a person may need to temporarily remove himself from all the demands of life. Sometimes I escape the pressures, abandon all of my responsibilities for a time, and then sit in the presence of God, letting Him bathe me in His grace.

This escaping and bathing are not possible for people until they are comfortable in God's love—until they can relax and not feel guilty, until they can enjoy doing nothing for a time and believe that during those moments of restoration God is just as pleased with them as when they are working very hard. Only then can a person relax and allow God's ministry of grace to flow into them.

The life of God flows into our very nature.
This life is the resurrection life of Jesus. The
same Spirit which resurrected Jesus from the
grave 2,000 years ago will resurrect our bodies of
death into bodies of life (Rom. 8:11).

Paul talks about this resurrection life in the
book of Ephesians. There he prays for the
Christians that they will understand three
things:

> *I pray that the eyes of your heart
> may be enlightened, so that you may
> know what is the hope of His calling,
> what are the riches of the glory of
> His inheritance in the saints, and
> what is the surpassing greatness of
> His power toward us who believe....*
>   (Eph. 1:18-19)

Pay special attention to the third thing which
Paul prayed for: that Christians will understand
the "power toward us who believe."

Right now there is power directed at you and
me. Paul prays that Christians will come to an
understanding of this power. He implies that the
eyes of our heart will have to be enlightened so
we can know it.

What is this power?

Paul goes on in Ephesians to explain:

> *...These are in accordance with the working of the strength of His might which He brought about in Christ, when He raised Him from the dead,....**   (Eph. 1:19-20)

Do you understand this? "Father, open their eyes." Realize that the same power which resurrected Jesus from the grave 2,000 years ago is directed toward you—right now.

---

* This passage goes on to tell of the ascension of Jesus which we will wait until chapter 30 to discuss.

Understanding the resurrection power of Jesus Christ was so profound and life-changing to Paul that he wrote:

> *...I count all things to be loss in view of the surpassing value of knowing Christ Jesus my Lord,...that I may know Him, and the power of His resurrection....* (Phil. 3:8-10)

Paul declared what is really important in life. After knowing Jesus, it's the power of Christ's resurrection—to know it and live in it.

This resurrection power is available both now and after we die. A day will come in the future when our mortal bodies will be transformed into glorified bodies. We will not see the fullness of that resurrection until the resurrection on the last day (I Cor. 15:35-52). However, we can experience that resurrection power today. Paul explained that he did not attain to the full resurrection while he was on this earth; however, he declared that he was experiencing it to some extent in his daily life, and he constantly was pressing on for a greater manifestation of it (Phil. 3:11-12).

Two thousand years ago, God looked down at His Son as He lay dead in the grave. Then the Father poured out His Spirit which brought life back into the Son. Think about this. That same resurrection power is directed toward you and me—right now.

As we live under grace, it is not just our mortal bodies which come to life. There is more to it than that. Paul explained:

> ...we believe that we shall also live with Him.   (Rom. 6:8)

We come to life. Furthermore, *Jesus comes to life within us.*

Picture our Lord Jesus dead in the grave 2,000 years ago. Think of Him arising. That is what happens inside of us. Jesus, Who lives within our inner man, resurrects to live within our whole being.

Paul explained the results which he experienced:

> *I have been crucified with Christ;*
> *and it is no longer I who live, but*
> *Christ lives in me....*   (Gal. 2:20)

This concept of Jesus living in us is not merely a figure of speech. It actually occurs. Jesus is alive in us now. He really is!

Remember what Paul taught us about our identification with Jesus in water baptism:

> *For if we have become united with*
> *Him in the likeness of His death,*
> *certainly we shall be also in the*
> *likeness of His resurrection.*
>
> > (Rom. 6:5)

This is not only for after we leave this earth. We can become united with His death and resurrection now.

When Jesus arises within us, His desires become our desires. His thoughts become our thoughts. His actions become our actions. His hands become our hands. Jesus will live in and through us when we live in His resurrection power.

The Christian who comes to understand this will be able to say:

"The life of Jesus is at work in me."
"His death is diminishing my old self."
"His resurrection power is transforming
   my body of death into a body of life."
"It is no longer I who live but Christ lives
   in me."

God has made this available to us by grace. I pray that the eyes of your heart will be enlightened. Grace is the transforming, resurrection power of God. It is directed toward you and me—right now.

People have a tendency to drift back under the law. They simply can't believe that the victorious life is as simple as letting Jesus resurrect in them.

Some will make a law out of anything. In fact, some Christians make a law out of the phrase, "walk according to the Spirit." Instead of seeing this as simply living under the constant flow of God's grace, they imagine it to be a difficult or even impossible task. They envision it as a struggle to hear what God is saying minute by minute and then forcing themselves to obey.

Of course, there is nothing wrong with attempting to know God's will; however, in Romans, chapter eight, we are being taught how to live under grace. To walk according to the Spirit in this context means to be in tune with the Spirit of Grace. It is to be bathed and nourished by the same Spirit which resurrected Jesus from the grave. To walk in the Spirit is to stay in step with the love and blessings which God is pouring out over you.

(For those of you who love animals, let me say that living in the Spirit is to be like a faithful dog bathing in the praise of his master. To be led by the Spirit is to be like a dog honored and overjoyed to walk next to His master.)

When we grasp this, we no longer see walking in the Spirit as a law. Basically it is letting God love us and empower us.

Christians also can make a law out of the phrase "set your mind on the Spirit." This phrase is used more than once in Romans, chapter eight, and it is key in understanding the victorious Christian life. However, some wrongly turn this into another law which they must obey.

To see how wrong this is, read Romans 8:5.

> *For those who are according to the flesh set their minds on the things of the flesh, but those who are according to the Spirit, the things of the Spirit.* (Rom. 8:5)

It is essential that you see the *cause* and the *effect* in this verse. We are told that if we are according to the flesh, then our minds will go on the things of the flesh. On the other hand, if we are according to the Spirit, our minds will go on the things of the Spirit.

CAUSE	EFFECT
According to the flesh——>	Mind on the flesh
According to the Spirit——>	Mind on the Spirit

Pay careful attention to this order. We are *not* being told to put our minds on the Spirit so that we can walk in the Spirit. It is the other way around. When we walk according to the Spirit, our minds—as a consequence—will be on the things of the Spirit.

This is so important, because many Christians wrongly conclude that they must control their mind, and then they make yet another law out of it.

In reality, Paul tells us that when a person is *according to the flesh*, it is impossible for him to control his mind. Of course, we can control our own minds in the sense of thinking about certain natural things; however, not in the sense of making our minds stay on the Spirit. Paul explained that a person who is according to the flesh *cannot* set his mind on the Spirit:

> *...because the mind set on the flesh is hostile toward God; for it does not subject itself to the law of God, for it is not even able to do so.* (Rom. 8:7)

We should not expect a person to put their mind on the Spirit until after they are *according to the Spirit*. In fact, it is impossible for them to do that.

The mind is not the control center of our being. Many Christians misunderstand this. They think that if they just can force their mind onto the things of God, then they will live in victory. That is untrue. You cannot control your mind truly unless you have been set free from the power of sin and death. Unless you are living under grace, you—including your mind—are enslaved to sin. Only after you move under grace can you set your mind on the things of the Spirit.

The control center of our being is, first of all, our heart. From the heart flow all the issues of life (Prov. 4:23). It is with our heart that we believe (Rom. 10:10). When we put our faith in Jesus Christ, we open our hearts to receive the grace which He is pouring out. That changes us. That sets us free.

Only then will our minds be free. Only then can our minds move unto the things of the Spirit. As the Spirit of God flows within us, our carnal thoughts change into holy thoughts. The degree to which we receive grace is the degree to which we can have the thoughts of God (I Cor. 2:12-16). As Jesus resurrects in us, we receive the mind of Christ. Hallelujah!

Then, if a negative thought comes to our mind we know that it is from the old, carnal nature. As new creatures in Christ, we can say, "That is not my thought. The old man died with Jesus." We do not need to claim those bad thoughts as ours. Nor do we need to fight them. As we see ourselves in the resurrection life of Jesus, unholy thoughts are washed away. New thoughts are born of the Spirit within us. Hence, we receive the mind of Christ.

Yes, the mind of Christ is a gift of God given to us by grace.

Grace is active, transforming, resurrection power. It motivates you, pushes you, and provides you with the power to control yourself.

For this reason, self-control is noted as one of the fruits of the Spirit (Gal. 5:22-23). Just as love and joy grow in the life of the Christian who allows the Spirit to fill them, so also does self-control.

Christians with the wrong definition of grace cannot understand this. If they still are thinking of grace as the opposite of law, then they will see grace as the *excuse* to *not* control nor govern themselves. On the other hand, if they truly understand that grace is God's power and love flowing from heaven toward them right now, then they will understand that grace is the *energy* and *reason* to control oneself.

Many Christians need a whole mind-renewing on this concept of self-control. Rather than seeing it as their enemy or a burden to bear, they need to see self-control as a wonderful, beautiful fruit of the Holy Spirit. The more a Christian is self-controlled, the more he is manifesting the nature of Jesus.

Earlier in Romans, chapter five, as Paul was beginning his teaching on the victorious Christian life, he wrote:

> ...*tribulation brings about perseverance, and perseverance, proven character; and proven character, hope; and hope does not disappoint....* (Rom.5:3-5)

Notice in these verses the progression in the life of the Christian.

"Tribulation" includes all the battles we face in life. In this passage Paul especially was referring to the temptations and sins with which we individually battle.

It is those battles which offer to us the path to proven character and hope. As a body builder lifts weights to increase the size of his muscles, we can resist sin and, hence, develop in character. As proven character grows, hope is produced. And hope does not disappoint, but leads to victory.

Yes, there is a war in the Christian life. A war where character is achieved. It is where the nature of Jesus is produced within us.

However, it is impossible to win without discovering the grace which flows from heaven. Immediately after the verses quoted above, Paul directs us back to this power, saying:

> *...because the love of God has been poured out within our hearts through the Holy Spirit who was given to us.*   (Rom. 5:5)

The power to overcome is in receiving God's love through the Holy Spirit.

Remember the story of Clare with her pet bird? (See chapter 12.) The bird was weak and sick until it came into the right environment. Once the bird got warm, it still had to get well. The bird still had to continue breathing. It had to get up off of the floor of the cage and get back on its perch. It needed to respond.

Sometimes responding to the love and grace of God can be a battle. Paul exhorts us in another passage:

> *Run in such a way that you may win. And everyone who competes in the games exercises self-control in all*

> things....I buffet my body and make
> it my slave, lest possibly, after I have
> preached to others, I myself should
> be disqualified.   (I Cor. 9:24b-27)

Self-control requires a mastery of one's own
appetites and desires. There is great reward for
this.

Paul explained this when He wrote that
perseverance produces proven character. As
character develops, hope grows. In contrast, the
person who does not persevere but, instead,
allows the trials, temptations, passions, and lusts
of life to overcome him repeatedly, grows
hopeless. The Christian who pushes back against
the negative pressures of life has his level of hope
increased day by day. Hope grows, and hope does
not disappoint but always leads to victory.

Just as love and joy are fruits of the Holy
Spirit, so also is self-control. We often recognize
love as beautiful, and we easily can see God's
nature being manifested when we observe
someone loving another person. With the exact
same clarity of thought, we must see self-control
as the expression of God in and through a person.
Self-control is beautiful. As a bodybuilder
develops his body until it appears as a sculpted
work of art, so also the person who has worked
against the forces of sin develops beautiful
character and self-control. He is a work of art—
God's art.

RECEIVE BY FAITH;
PERFECTED BY FAITH

How do we obtain the power needed to overcome sin? How can we access the Spirit? This is the question Paul tried to answer for the Christians in Galatia:

> *...did you receive the Spirit by works of the Law, or by hearing with faith?*
> (Gal. 3:2)

Paul reminded the Christians that they first received the Holy Spirit by simply believing in Him when they heard about Him. In the exact same way—by hearing with faith—we continue to receive the Spirit.

God

Jesus

Receive by Faith

We cannot earn the Holy Spirit. There are no set of rules or requirements which we must fulfill before the Holy Spirit is poured into us. The Holy Spirit is being poured out on our behalf. He flows by God's grace.

When we hear, we believe, and we receive.

Paul added to the verse we last quoted, saying:

> *Are you so foolish? Having begun by the Sprit, are you now being perfected by the flesh?* (Gal. 3:3)

Obviously, we will be perfected the same way we began in the Christian walk. We will continue to receive the Spirit by hearing and believing.

Right now you are *hearing*. I have been telling you about the power which flows from heaven. You are making a decision this very instant to receive or reject that power. You hear, you believe, you receive.

In the beginning of Romans, Paul made a statement that brings everything into perspective:

> *For I am not ashamed of the gospel, for it is the power of God for salvation to everyone who believes....*
> (Rom. 1:16)

Where is the power of God? It is in the gospel. The power of God *is* the good news.

For whom will the power of God be available? For everyone who believes the good news. As they receive the good news, they receive the power.

We know this is true concerning our initial salvation experience when we find forgiveness of sins. We hear the gospel and we believe. The gospel *is* the power of God released into our lives to reconcile us to God and make us His children.

That is exciting, but I want you to see the gospel as more than that. Too often Christians today see salvation merely as being saved from damnation to hell. But in the Bible, salvation is much more than that. It includes all areas of life. In the context of Romans five through eight, Paul was teaching how the Christian can be saved from the power of sin and death. This is the emphasis of salvation which I hope you can grasp: you can be saved from the power of sin by receiving the Spirit of Grace.

Paul wrote that the gospel is the power of God for salvation, then he quoted a passage from the Old Testament which says:

> *"But the righteous man shall live by faith."* (Rom. 1:17b)

Martin Luther read these words five centuries ago and came to the conclusion that man is saved from damnation by putting his faith in Jesus Christ. That concept has been a foundational truth of the Christian faith ever since.

Today, I am asking you to see those words as applicable not only to your salvation from hell, but also as a promise for power to live. Again:

> *"But the righteous man shall <u>live</u> by faith."*
> (Rom. 1:17b, emphasis added)

Not only will we be saved from damnation, but we also will live victoriously by putting our faith in Jesus Christ.

Jesus not only died for you, He also lives for you. You can receive both forgiveness of sins and freedom from sin. His death provides forgiveness of sins; His life provides power over sin.

Salvation from hell is a free gift of God. So is victory over sin. Just as you receive one by faith, so you receive the other by faith. I have good news and I am not ashamed of it. The good news is the power of God to all who believe. I am communicating to you the good news right now. Receive the good news and you receive the power. God loves you. His grace is flowing toward you. I pray the eyes of your heart will be enlightened. The same power which resurrected Jesus from the grave is directed toward you right now. Live by faith.

Receiving the Spirit of Grace by faith promises to us more than freedom from sin. Paul told us that if we "receive the abundance of grace and of the gift of righteousness we will reign in life through the One Jesus Christ" (Rom. 5:17). I want to reign in life. Don't you?

This reigning power becomes evident as we identify not only the resurrection power of Jesus, but also His ascension power.

Earlier, we quoted Paul's words on the power directed toward us—the same power which resurrected Jesus from the grave. However, it was more than resurrection power. It was also the power which caused our Lord to ascend far above all rule and authority.

Paul prayed that the eyes of your heart might be enlightened, that:

> *...you might know what is...the surpassing greatness of His power toward us who believe. These are in accordance with the working of the strength of His might which He brought about in Christ, when He raised Him from the dead, and seated Him at His right hand in the heavenly places, far above all rule*

*and authority and power and
dominion....* (Eph. 1:18-21)

Think about it. Two thousand years ago, God the Father looked down at His Son Who had been crucified. By the power of the Spirit, God raised the Son to life. But He did not stop there. He elevated Him to the throne. This was not simply lifting His body into the heavens, but a great exertion of power as everything in existence was forced under our Lord's feet.

This same power is directed toward us.

Ascension power is different than resurrection power. It lifts us to a place of authority. Paul said that as a consequence of this ascension power, God has:

*...raised us up with Him, and seated
us with Him in the heavenly places,
in Christ Jesus.* (Eph. 2:6)

Many Christians think verses like this are merely figures of speech or promises to be fulfilled in the future. Again, I pray that the eyes of your heart will be opened.

The same power which elevated Jesus far above all rule and authority is directed toward you and me right now. As we receive grace, ascension power lifts us. It lifts us above trials, obstacles, temptations, and attacks of the enemy. It places those things under our feet. Ascension power causes us to reign in life.

This is not merely some mystical experience. It can be reality in your life.

I shared how God freed me from years of tormenting thoughts. Part of that victory came through believing in the ascension power of Jesus. I discovered my life being guided down a new path. I started meeting the right people at the right time. Helpful information came into my hands. My steps seemed to be guided down the path to victory, one step at a time. The ascension power of Jesus began orchestrating my life toward the goal of freedom.

The ascension power not only helped me overcome sin, but today it allows me to fulfill God's plan for my life. As I attempt to do all God has called me to do, I allow Him to open doors on my behalf, take me where He wants me to go, give me authority to speak to influential people, show me where to locate necessary provisions, and guide me to walk out His plan for my life.

Jesus who lives inside of us is victorious. He reigns. In His presence every knee bows. As we allow His presence to rise in us, obstacles bow. The path to fulfill His will opens before us. The same power which elevated Him 2,000 years ago, and now causes all things to bow in His presence, will cause things to bow before us.

Now, when I am faced by a difficult situation, I consciously allow the ascension power of our Lord to flow through me. I receive grace by faith. As Jesus rises in me, His ascension power flows. Things around me gradually come into alignment with the will of God.

For example, if there is some person to whom I know I should talk, but I have not had the opportunity, I consciously receive God's grace. I know His grace flowing through me will open the right doors and make the opportunity come about. Somehow, at the right time, in the right place, God will ordain the encounter, and soon that person and I will be standing in front of one another. I have seen the ascension power of Jesus work in this fashion repeatedly.

Ascension Power

Circumstances, Events, Trials, Temptations, Obstacles, Satan.

I have an advantage over the non-Christian. I have ascension power at work in me and through me. I count all things but loss in view of the surpassing greatness of knowing Him and the power of His ascension. He has enabled me to reign.

This is why Paul can say boldly in Romans 8:28:

> *And we know that God causes all things to work together for good to those who love God, to those who are called according to His purpose.*

As you walk according to the Spirit—according to the Spirit of Grace being poured out from heaven—all things work together. Just as God *causes you to obey*, so also He will *cause all things to work for good*.

Change may not come instantaneously, but it will come. Everyone faces difficulties. Trials are a part of life. However, the Christian has resurrection power available which gives hope and spiritual life in the midst of difficulties. Furthermore, the ascension power of Jesus Christ flows causing all things to move into alignment with the perfect will of God.

The Christian who understands this will wait on God and allow God's grace to flow. The Apostle Paul knew and demonstrated this. One time he stepped out to preach the gospel in the city of Macedonia, but the people did not receive him.

Instead, he was beaten and locked in the bottom of a prison. There he began to praise God and soon the prison doors opened. The manager of the prison responded to the gospel, and, in time, even the leaders of the city came to respect Paul (Acts 16:9-40). The apostle understood what the ascension of Jesus Christ means for us: prison doors will open and that which opposes God eventually will bow.

Two thousand years ago the ascension power of God put everything under the feet of our Lord Jesus. That same power is flowing toward you and me. I pray that the eyes of your heart may be opened. If we believe, then the ascension power of Jesus Christ will flow through our lives, causing things to move under our feet.

For this reason Paul could say confidently in the end of the book of Romans:

> *And the God of peace will soon crush*
> *Satan under your feet. The grace of*
> *our Lord Jesus be with you.*
> (Rom. 16:20)

Parting Blessing

It is time to let God bless you. Open your heart and receive the grace He is pouring out in abundance. Now let the nature of Jesus Christ resurrect in you. Come forth man of God. Arise woman of God. Ascend! The grace of God is flowing toward you right now. Bathe in His grace. Stay in His love. Cultivate this as a lifestyle.

THE COMPLETE WINESKIN (Fourth edition)

The Body of Christ is in a reformation. God is pouring out the Holy Spirit and our wineskins must be changed to handle the new wine. Will the Church come together in unity? Where do small group meetings fit? How does the anointing of God work and what is your role? What is the 5-fold ministry? How are apostles, prophets, evangelists, pastors and teachers going to rise up and work together? This book puts into words what you have been sensing in your spirit. (Eberle's best seller, translated into many languages, distributed worldwide.)

Who Is God?

This is an in-depth teaching on the nature of God and it implications on our understanding of humanity. This book is radical, bold and captivating, yet already has the endorsements of the some of the most influential Christian leaders in the world. As C. P. Wagner has written, "This thrilling theology!" This book is soon to be released in hard copy, but presently you can download it from the web site of Worldcast Publishing:

www.worldcastpublihsing.com

TWO BECOME ONE (Second edition)

Releasing God's Power for Romance, Sexual Freedom
and Blessings in Marriage

Kindle afresh the "buzz of love." Find out how to make God's law of binding forces work for you instead of against you. The keys to a thrilling, passionate, and fulfilling marriage can be yours if you want them. This book is of great benefit to pastors, counselors, young singles, divorcees and especially married people. Couples are encouraged to read it together.

GOD'S LEADERS FOR TOMORROW'S WORLD

(Revised/expanded edition) You sense a call to leadership in your life, but questions persist: "Does God want me to rise up? Is this pride? Do I truly know where to lead? How can I influence people?" Through a new understanding of leadership dynamics, learn how to develop godly charisma. Confusion will melt into order when you see the God-ordained lines of authority. Fear of leadership will change to confidence as you learn to handle power struggles. Move into your "metron," that is, your God-given authority.

GRACE...THE POWER TO REIGN

The Light Shining from Romans 5-8

We struggle against sin and yearn for God's highest. Yet, on a bad day it is as as if we are fighting with gravity. Our questions go unanswered:

- Where is the power to overcome temptations and trials?
- Is God really willing to breathe into us so that these dry bones can live and we may be victorious?

For anyone who ever has clenched his or her fist in the struggle to live godly, here are the answers. Just as there is a force in the world pushing us to sin, there is a greater force flowing from God which can lift us, transform us, and make us what He wants us to be. It is grace! It is grace which few have grasped, yet, so many have sought desperately. Now you can find it.

IF GOD IS GOOD,
WHY IS THERE SO MUCH SUFFERING AND PAIN?

Life isn't fair! Terrorist bombings. Ethnic cleansing. Body-ravaging diseases. Murder. Child abuse. Natural disasters. Genetic maladies. These travesties, global and seemingly relentless, drive us to the limits of our reasoning. When pain and suffering invade our well-laid plans for a good life, we ask the gut question: Why, God, why? In this book, Harold R. Eberle evaluates the role God plays in the Earth, explores the origin of suffering, and reassures us of God kind intentions toward us.

DEVELOPING A PROSPEROUS SOUL
VOL I: HOW TO OVERCOME A POVERTY MIND-SET
VOL II: HOW TO MOVE INTO
GOD'S FINANCIAL BLESSINGS

There are fundamental changes you can make in the way you think which will help release God's blessings. This is a balanced look at the promises of God with practical steps you can take to move into financial freedom. It is time for Christians to recapture the financial arena.

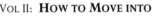
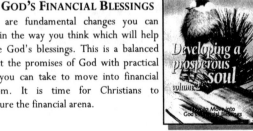

VICTORIOUS ESCHATOLOGY (Second edition)

A Partial Preterist View
Co-authored by Harold R. Eberle and Martin Trench

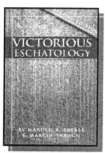

A biblically-based, optimistic view of the future. Along with a historical perspective, Harold R. Eberle and Martin Trench present a clear understanding of Matthew 24, the book of Revelation, and other key passages about the events to precede the return of Jesus Christ. Satan is not going to take over this world. Jesus Christ is Lord and He will reign until every enemy is put under His feet!

YOU SHALL RECEIVE POWER

Moving Beyond Pentecostal & Charismatic Theology

God's Spirit will fill you in measures beyond what you are experiencing presently. This is not just about Pentecostal or Charismatic blessings. There is something greater. It is for all Christians, and it will build a bridge between those Christians who speak in tongues and those who do not. It is time for the whole Church to take a fresh look at the work of the Holy Spirit in our individual lives. This book will help you. It will challenge you, broaden your perspective, set you rejoicing, fill you with hope, and leave you longing for more of God.

PRECIOUS IN HIS SIGHT *A Fresh Look at the Nature of Man* During the Fourth and Fifth Centuries Augustine taught about the nature of humanity using as his key Scripture a verse in the book of Romans which had been mistranslated. Since that time the Church has embraced a false concept of humanity which has negatively influenced every area of Christianity. It is time for Christians to come out of darkness! This book, considered by many to be Harold Eberle's greatest work, has implications upon our understanding of sin, salvation, who God is, evangelism, the world around us and how we can live the daily, victorious lifestyle.

To place an order or to check current prices call:
1-800-308-5837 within the USA or:
509-248-5837 from outside the USA

Worldcast Publishing
P.O. Box 10653
Yakima, WA 98909-1653

E-mail: office@worldcastpublishing.com
Web Site: www.worldcastpublishing.com